50 JOKES

by AVA

By Marissa & Ava Trainor
Illustrated by Jonathan Fackler

MW01147671

50 Jokes by Ava

Copyright 2021 by Marissa and Ava Trainor

ISBN 978-1-945169-67-0

Illustrations by Jonathan Fackler

All Rights Reserved. No part of this book may be reproduced or transmitted in any form or by any means, electronic or mechanical, including photocopying, recording, or by any information storage and retrieval system without written permission from the author, except for the inclusion of brief quotations in a review.

Orison Publishers, Inc.
PO Box 188, Grantham, PA 17027
717-731-1405
www.OrisonPublishers.com
Publish your book now,
marsha@orisonpublishers.com

This book is dedicated to
Ava's dad, Ed,
who always finds a way
to brighten our day
with his
awesome sense of humor.

What type
of bug has
the best manners?

Lady-bug.

Q. What kind of bow
can't be tied?
A. A Rain-bow!

Q. How did the quarterback
cool off after the game?
A. He went to sit with the fans.

Q. What did the cat say
when she saw the dog?
A. Get Me-owt!

Q. What is the astronaut's
favorite dessert?
A. A Moon Pie.

Laughter is the shortest distance between two people.

Victor Borge

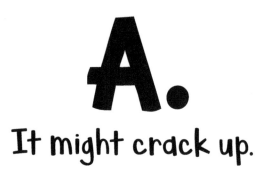

Q.

Why can't the egg
laugh at the chicken?

A.

It might crack up.

Q. What is a cat's favorite snack?

A. Cat-vi-ar!

Q. What kind of soup do you eat when you visit France?

A. French Onion.

Q. Why did the jelly go to the party?

A. Because it was time to jam.

Q. Why did the student bring a ladder to school?

A. Because he wanted a higher education.

Laughter is
an instant vacation.

Milton Berle

Q.

What did the pie
say to the fly
that landed on it?

A.

Shoo-fly!

Q. Why do onions avoid the sun?

A. Because they peel.

Q. What type of pizza does a computer like best?

A. Pizza Bytes!

Q. What did Elsa say to Anna after she built a snowman?

A. That was snow much fun!

Q. What do you call a girl standing in the middle of a tennis court?

A. Annette.

Laughter is the sound of the soul dancing.

Jarod Kintz

What is a cow's
favorite type of cheese?

Moo-zarella!

Q. What is a puppy's favorite snack?

A. Pupperoni!

Q. How did we know that seven was hungry?

A. Because seven-eight-nine!

Q. What did the egg say after he watched his favorite movie?

A. That was EGG-cellent!

Q. Where did the dog go to celebrate?

A. A paw-ty!

A day without laughter
is a day wasted.

Charlie Chaplan

Q.

Why does the sneaker
love music?

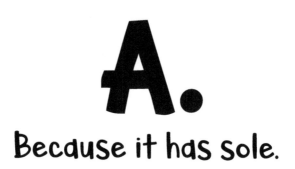

Because it has sole.

Q. Why did the octopus win the fight?

A. Because she was well-armed.

Q. Why did the jalapeno go to the nurse?

A. Because it was feeling hot.

Q. What did the pan eat on its birthday?

A. Pancakes!

Q. Why did the firefly fail his science test?

A. Because he wasn't very bright.

Laughter is timeless, imagination has no age, dreams are forever.

Walt Disney

Q.

What is a pirate's
favorite state to visit?

A.

Aaarrrkansas!

Q. What type of cheese is really sad?
A. Blue cheese

Q. Why doesn't Grandma like sugar with her coffee?
A. Because she is already sweet enough!

Q. What do sleepy cats like to do?
A. Take a cat-nap.

Q. Where do fish go to take a vacation?
A. Fin-land.

Life is better
when you're laughing.

Snoopy

Q.

What is a baker's
favorite thing to do?

A.

Loaf around.

Q. Why was the stomach afraid?

A. Because it didn't have any guts.

Q. What is Elsa's favorite game to play?

A. Freeze Tag!

Q. What part of a donut is fat-free?

A. The center.

Q. Why was the sheep tired?

A. Because it jumped over the moon so many times!

Laughter is
the best medicine
in the world.

Milton Berle

What type of cat
can swim?

A Cat-fish!

Q. What is a ghost's favorite type of pie?

A. Booberry.

Q. What type of music does a bunny like best?

A. Hip-hop!

Q. What does a polar bear eat for breakfast?

A. Ice Krispies

Knock, knock.
Who's there?
May.
May who?
May The Force Be With You!

Laughter is a
sunbeam of the soul.

Thomas Mann

Q.

Who brought the puppy a present?

A.

Santa-paws!

Q. How does the ocean say goodbye?

A. It waves.

Q. What type of cat do you see on Halloween?

A. A scaredy cat!

Q. What is a goblin's favorite food?

A. Ghoulash!

Q. Why did the salad go to the recording studio?

A. To get some beets.

There is nothing in the world so irresistibly contagious as laughter and good humor.

Charles Dickens

Q.

**Why did the squirrel
go crazy?**

A.

It ate too many nuts!

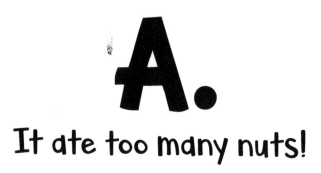

Q. What did the 1st astronaut say to the 2nd astronaut?

A. That trip was out-of-this-world!

Q. What was the bat's favorite sport?

A. Baseball!

Q. What is a bee's favorite type of cereal?

A. Honey Comb.

Q. How does a cloud wipe the snow off its windshield?

A. It uses a skyscraper.

Against the assault
of laughter,
nothing can stand.

Mark Twain

CPSIA information can be obtained
at www.ICGtesting.com
Printed in the USA
LVHW021152171121
703473LV00010B/628

9 781945 169670